PENGUIN BOOKS

YOUR MOTHER IS A REMARKABLE WOMAN

S. Gross has been drawing cartoons for over thirty years, and he's going to keep on drawing them until he gets them right. Before he was born he wanted to be Shirley MacLaine, but that was already taken so he had to settle for growing up in the Bronx, acquiring a horrendous accent, and having a life-long resentment against Chang and Eng, who not only became Shirley MacLaine but also Magda Lupescu.

In addition to being a cartoonist, Mr. Gross is also the Pretender to the throne of Ruthenia and frequently has fantasies about the thrones of Saxe-Coburg-Gotha and Aragon. His motto is *Ad Astra per Yux.*

Your Mother Is a Remarkable Woman

S. GROSS

PENGUIN BOOKS

PENGUIN BOOKS
Published by the Penguin Group
Viking Penguin, a division of Penguin Books USA Inc.,
375 Hudson Street, New York, New York 10014, U.S.A.
Penguin Books Ltd, 27 Wrights Lane, London W8 5TZ, England
Penguin Books Australia Ltd, Ringwood, Victoria, Australia
Penguin Books Canada Ltd, 10 Alcorn Avenue, Suite 300,
Toronto, Ontario, Canada M4V 3B2
Penguin Books (N.Z.) Ltd, 182–190 Wairau Road,
Auckland 10, New Zealand

Penguin Books Ltd, Registered Offices:
Harmondsworth, Middlesex, England

First published in Penguin Books 1992

1   3   5   7   9   10   8   6   4   2

Some of the cartoons in this collection were first published in *The New Yorker* and are reproduced
with permission. Other cartoons have appeared in the following publications: *American Health,
Audubon, Cosmopolitan, Diversion, Funnnies, Good Housekeeping, Gourmet, Harvard Business
Review, Inside Books, Manhattan Inc., MTV to Go, National Lampoon, The New York Times Book
Review, OBG Management, Lears, Parenting, Playboy Deutschland, Psychology Today, Quark Maga-
zine, Science Digest, Seven, Soundings, Special Reports, Teenage,* and *Woman's World.*

LIBRARY OF CONGRESS CATALOGING IN PUBLICATION DATA
Gross, S. (Sam)
Your mother is a remarkable woman/ S. Gross.
p.   cm.
ISBN 0 14 01.5608 9
1. Women—Caricatures and cartoons.   2. American wit and humor,
Pictorial.   I. Title.
NC1429.G76A4   1992
741.5'973—dc20   91–39037

Printed in the United States of America

Set in Clearface Regular
Designed by Kathryn Parise

"Son, your mother is a remarkable woman."

S. GROSS

"Hey, that's not fair! You're using Japanese money!"

"What a humiliation! The Home Economics Department beat us in the race to create life!"

"Quick! Follow that dish and spoon!"

S.GROSS

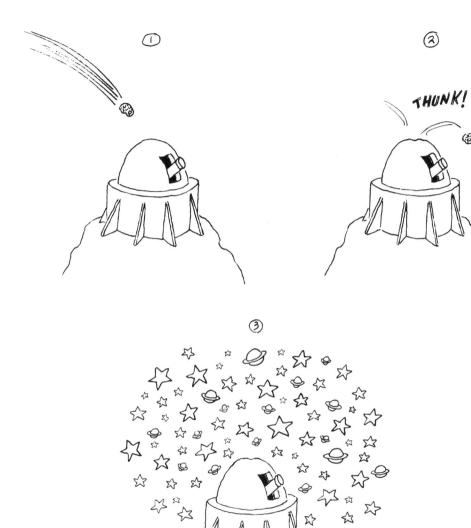

THUNK!

© 1973 The New Yorker Magazine, Inc.

"I'm thinking of having her declawed."

© 1990 The New Yorker Magazine, Inc.

"We also sell compact discs."

"You colorized 'Casablanca.' How unfortunate."

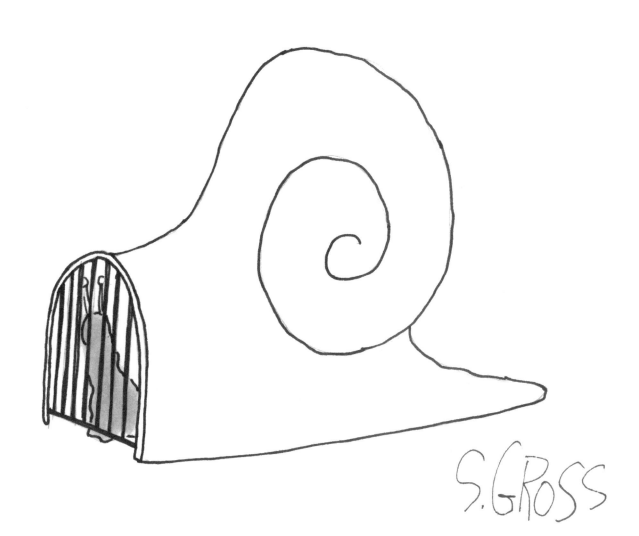

S.GROSS

"It's just my initial impression . . . he looks nurturing."

HOT CHESTNUTS

S.GROSS

"There used to be an eighth dwarf, Humpy, but he left rather suddenly."

S. GROSS

"Life is a cabaret, and you're not going to get in."

"My wife doesn't understand me."

S.GROSS

"You can't fool me. You're a worm."

S.GROSS

"Yes, son, it's true. You were adopted."

"If that's the commissioner, tell him I'm not in."

"At least he let us keep the T-shirts."

S.GROSS

YOU ARE NOW
LEAVING
HITHER
AND ENTERING
YON

S. GROSS

"Damn it, Gundleman! You're not taking this experiment seriously."

S.GROSS

"I'll take it. Charge it to Beatrix Potter's account."

S. GROSS

"Let me through! I'm an upholsterer!"

"Wow! It's David and Lisa, my hamsters!"

S. GROSS

"Santa's not coming, and I'm the one who puts lumps of coal in your stocking."

"Come on in, the tar's fine!"

S. GROSS

"If you're so enlightened, how come you can't lick that slice?"

"We interrupt this program to bring you an important bulletin. . . .
There's a dead mouse in the wall behind the piano."

S. GROSS

"We need something with high ceilings."

"You have nice legs."

"We're hoping for a really smooth wine here."

S.GROSS

"And now here's Zeus with the weather."

"I understand walking is very good exercise."

"Now that you're finished with her, could you turn my mushroom into a three-bedroom colonial with a sunken living room and a wood-burning fireplace?"

S.GROSS

"Now go out and win one for the guppy!"

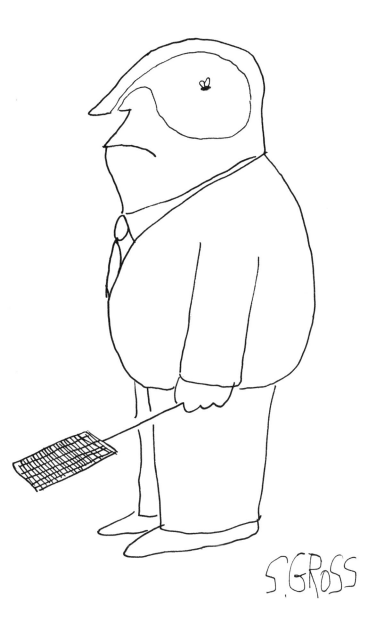

"The trouble with you is that you treat love as if it were a joke."

S.GROSS

"I want to be kosher."

S. GROSS

S. GROSS

"Does that include cats?"

"I'm it. There was a crack-down by the humane society."

S. GROSS

"Help! I can't pay the rent!"

THESE CRUMBS ARE BROUGHT TO YOU BY A GRANT FROM THE SAMUEL R. HENNING FOUNDATION

S. GROSS

"You're never going to make it to Florida loaded up like that."

S.GROSS

S.GROSS

"The French consider him a creative genius."

"Gimme a worm and I'll bring your boat in."

"I love your nose."

S. GROSS

"I'm afraid it's too late. His heart has stopped bleeding."

"Report to the infirmary. You look like you're coming down with something.'

S.GROSS

"Your husband went back to his first wife and is already on board."

S. GROSS

S. GROSS

TYPE-A
PERSONALITY

NEXT
TANTRUM

3PM

S.GROSS

"When we write up the gospels, let's not mention that he had a pet fish."

S.GROSS

S.GROSS

"I'm trying to forget about a girl, but it's hard. Her name is Sandy."

S.GROSS

"This is going to sound silly, but you're going to marry a pussycat."

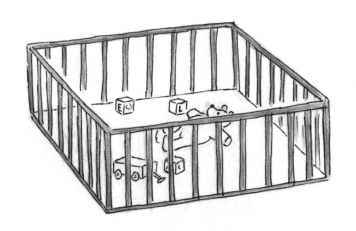

S.GROSS

"Sorry about this,
    but I just ran out of sand."

S. GROSS

"I just figured out the meaning of life: water!"

"I think I have a right to know. Who's Clara?"

"Hey, you guys were terrific!"

"You certainly know how to show a girl a good time!"

S.GROSS

①

②

S.GROSS

THIS SECTION CLOSED

S.GROSS

"I read somewhere that when two people live together for a long time they start to look like each other."

S.GROSS

TIME
1:32
TEMP
60°
SOUP OF
THE DAY
ONION

S.GROSS

"How about a Shirley Temple on the house and then you skedaddle."

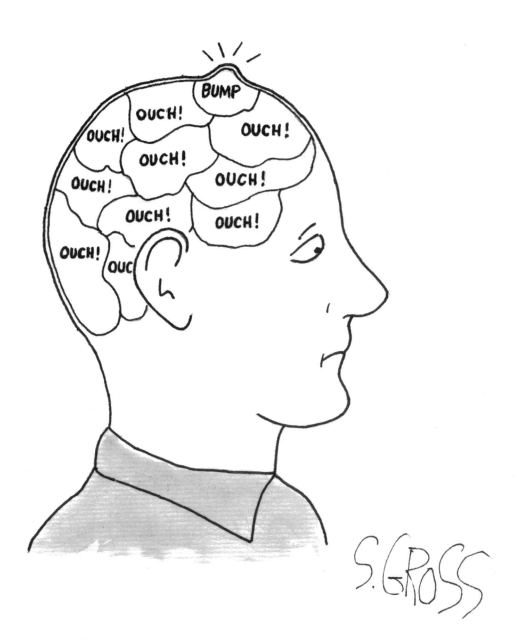

"How much for the plant?"

"It's things like this that give boxing a bad name."

S.GROSS

"Mom baby!"

"Doctor, this is Mr. Gusset. Mr. Gusset thinks he's the Empire State Building."

"I suggest that we grab a bite first."

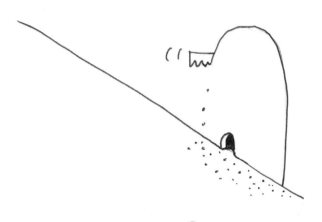

S.GROSS

"He didn't listen to his mommy and he went and played in a tar pit."

"Romulus is going to found Rome and Remus is going to be a businessman."

S.GROSS

"Good Heavens! Who hooked you up? This one is Cable-TV!"

"You're playing with your food again, Eugene!"

S.GROSS

S.GROSS

"Remember, he likes to be called 'Chief.'"

S.GROSS

"Do you have
'The Joy of Begging for Sex'?"

S. GROSS

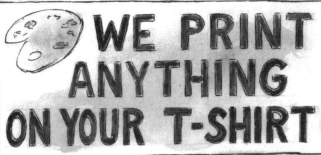

"Before you change me into a real boy, what about my girlfriend?"

"Let's hope it's an isolated frog and not another plague."

S.GROSS

"I'm her secretary.
What do you want?"

"You'll have to hang in there a little longer.
The government is investigating the contractor."

"If you decide to take it, we can have it ready for occupancy by late October."

"First of all, I just bumped my head."

"Did you get a smell of her feet?"

S.GROSS

S. GROSS

"Darling, we can't go on meeting like this. My husband is starting to get suspicious."

S.GROSS

"Hi. I'm the lost sock fairy. You dropped this at the laundromat."

"This is merely a registration just in case we have to call you up at a later date."

S. GROSS

"If that's Grandpa, tell him I've already left."

POET'S CORNER

EXIT

S.GROSS

"God, I hate commuting!"

S.GROSS